Original title:
Breathe Green

Copyright © 2025 Creative Arts Management OÜ
All rights reserved.

Author: Christian Leclair
ISBN HARDBACK: 978-1-80581-886-1
ISBN PAPERBACK: 978-1-80581-413-9
ISBN EBOOK: 978-1-80581-886-1

Whispers in the Wind

In a park where the squirrels dance,
A leaf flew by, it took a chance.
A pigeon laughed, then let out a squawk,
"You're just a leaf, you can't even talk!"

The daisies wiggled, feeling spry,
They giggled loud as a butterfly.
"Look at that branch, so stiff and proud!"
"You need a disco, not a crowd!"

The sun peeked through with a wink so sly,
A cloud said, "Wait, I'm going to cry!"
But then it chuckled, puffy and round,
"I'll shower you gently, don't hit the ground!"

A worm in the soil just wiggled along,
"Nature's a dance, can't I join the song?"
The grass whispered back, in rhythm so keen,
"You're the twist in my groove, if you know what I mean!"

Lush Embrace of Life

In the garden, things get silly,
While worms wiggle, oh so frilly.
The daisies giggle, the roses dance,
As squirrels wear hats and prance.

Bees with ties are buzzing loud,
While ants perform for the crowd.
Nature throws a grand ol' ball,
And everyone's invited, big and small!

Exhaled Leaves

Leaves fall down with a twisty twirl,
Spinning like a dizzy girl.
Crickets chatter in funny tones,
While spiky thistles shake their bones.

The trees wear shades, very chic,
Whispering secrets, oh so sneak.
Underneath, a rabbit hops,
Collecting acorns, never stops!

Chasing Chlorophyll Dreams

In a meadow where gnomes play,
Chasing shadows through the day.
Caterpillars dance a waltz,
While ladybugs shout, 'It's not our fault!'

The grasshoppers sing with flair,
Making music that's quite rare.
A dandelion, bold and spry,
Winks at the sun, oh my, oh my!

Nature's Gentle Lullaby

Crickets strum on tiny strings,
While trees sway and softly sing.
The moon peeks through leafy crowns,
As frogs in capes leap all around.

A gentle breeze tells silly tales,
Of snails in boats and fish with scales.
And as the stars begin to blink,
The world laughs and starts to think!

Verdant Reflections

In a world of leafy pranks,
The trees wear belts, the shrubs wear tanks.
Squirrels throw acorns with flair and spins,
While grasshoppers dance with wild, silly grins.

Sunflowers gossip, sharing the tea,
About the daisies who fell from the bee.
A worm in a tie sings a tune of cheer,
While mushrooms groove, hopping around like a deer.

The Forest's Heartbeat

The woods are alive, with laughter and cheers,
A fox in a tux, wiping down his spears.
The owls pretend to be wise and profound,
Yet trip over branches, just tumbling down.

The woodpecker drums to a ridiculous beat,
While raccoons hold court with their garbage feast.
A butterfly brings popcorn, spreading it wide,
As the party of foliage swells up with pride.

Overlapping Canopies

Canopies clash in a playful fight,
With leaves casting shadows and tickling light.
A twig gossips secrets to ferns all around,
As mushrooms declare they're the kings of the ground.

Up top, the birds hold a wild karaoke,
With worms as the judges, oh how they can be!
Hilarity grows, with rumbles and shakes,
As nature sings songs that can make the earth quake.

Nature's Breath of Freshness

The breeze brought a joke, floating through the pines,
It tickled the flowers, who laughed at the lines.
A bee wears a hat, sipping nectar with style,
While a turtle explains how to run a short mile.

Giggling grasses sway in a comical waltz,
As nearby a lizard declares, 'No defaults!'
When the sun sets to close this whimsical day,
Nature's own laughter just lightens the way.

Inhale the Wilderness

In the forest, I took a gulp,
A squirrel laughed, what a lumpy pulp!
The trees swayed, doing a jig,
While I sneezed like a big old pig.

Mushrooms danced, wearing silly hats,
As I tripped on the roots, oh those bratty spats!
Chasing butterflies, oh what a sight,
They tickled my nose, oh what a fright!

A Chorus of Fresh Air

The flowers sang a silly tune,
While bees bustled 'round like a cartoon.
A breeze blew, and the trees all laughed,
While I gasped at the scent of fresh daft!

The grass sprouted feet, tapping away,
As I joined in the dance, oh what a day!
With giggles of clouds drifting by,
I waved at the sky, oh my oh my!

Green Hues of Serenity

The ferns threw a party, in shades of lime,
They called out to me, saying, 'You're just in time!'
A ladybug winked, wearing shades of red,
While I marveled at the garden they bred.

With laughter, the bushes held a game,
As I bounced and tumbled—oh, what a shame!
The daisies chuckled as I fell down,
While nature's giggles twirled all around.

The Sigh of the Earth

The earth lets out a hearty grunt,
As worms squirm and caterpillars hunt.
Oh, what a ruckus, the ground does make,
With roots tickling toes, oh for goodness' sake!

Moss cushions all, like a plushy bed,
As I snore lightly, 'neath leafy spreads.
The rocks roll their eyes, and the soil just sighs,
Nature's a jester, in disguise!

The Exhale of Eden

In the garden of giggles, plants sway,
Laughing at butterflies, on their way.
The daisies dance, on the ground they prance,
While dandelions puff in a wild romance.

Squirrels wear shades, looking quite sly,
They've got the sun's bling, oh my, oh my!
Chasing down acorns like they're lost treasures,
In this sunny place, they measure their pleasures.

Chasing Dappled Light

Sunbeams are taggers, they zip and they zoom,
As shadows play hide-and-seek with a broom.
A wobbly worm does the twist on the trail,
While leaves cackle softly, telling a tale.

A bird in a hat sings a tune so absurd,
Possessing a flair, that's utterly blurred.
The laughter of echoes makes giggles collide,
In the sunlight, all secrets are destined to hide.

Serenade of Sun-kissed Leaves

Wise old trees gossip, in rustling tones,
Whispering secrets of sticks and of stones.
A squirrel's tail twirls in a zany stunt,
While mushrooms throw parties at the roots of the front.

Sunlight dabs colors, on everything near,
A worm spoofs the grass, with impressive cheer.
Polka-dot petals prance, full of delight,
As bees do the cha-cha, buzzing in flight.

Ballet of Blossoms

Tulips take center stage, twirling in line,
While daisies do ballet, so sleek and divine.
Their pirouettes sparkle in glittery rain,
As violets chuckle, feeling no pain.

A hedgehog in tights steals the show with a bow,
With an encore of snorts, as only he could allow.
The meadow's a stage, wild and full of grace,
Flora takes flight, in a whimsical race.

Whispers of the Verdant

In a garden that giggles with beings so sly,
The flowers wear glasses, and daisies can lie.
A squirrel with a mustache steals snacks all around,
While worms sing their songs underground without sound.

The grass blades are gossiping, swaying with glee,
The tulips in tutus put on quite a spree.
Bees in their bowties serve honey on toast,
While worms dance the tango, now aren't they a host?

Lungs of the Forest

The trees are all coughing, or so it would seem,
They exhale with hiccups, a comical theme.
A raccoon on a branch is auditioning scenes,
While owls wear scarves, their wisdom to glean.

The pines are all whispering jokes in a line,
As chipmunks throw acorns like they're on a dime.
A bear wears a beanie, he's hip, oh so cool,
And the brook giggles past, like it's breaking a rule.

Symphony of Leaves

The leaves clap together, a comical tune,
As frogs on a lily sing out 'Not so soon!'
With toads in tuxedos, they're holding a play,
While crickets start tap dancing, come join the ballet.

The wind is the conductor with wild, crazy hair,
While squirrels in jackets are soaring through air.
The rustling of bushes joins in with a cheer,
Nature's grand concert brings laughter, oh dear!

Echoes in the Canopy

The branches are chatting, what tales do they spin?
The owls say 'Hoo!' while the raccoons grin.
Monkeys in goggles attempt some cool tricks,
While sprightly young leaves play their funny little flicks.

The moss on the ground is holding a ball,
While ferns do the limbo, standing proud and tall.
With bats wearing capes, flying high without care,
Echoes of laughter float free in the air.

Awakening in the Arboretum

In the trees where squirrels play,
Chasing leaves that float away.
A gopher sneezes, gives a shout,
"Why's the grass always in a drought?"

Dandelions giggle, dance with glee,
"We're not weeds, we're wild and free!"
The sun winks down on this delight,
And bees are buzzing, what a sight!

A hedgehog rolls, thinks he's a ball,
While mushrooms plan a crazy crawl.
With every step, the earth does cheer,
The laughter whispers, loud and clear.

Air Infused with Life

A raccoon dons a little hat,
Claims the air smells just like chat.
"Who knew?" he snickers with a tilt,
"Nature's gossip? That's my quilt!"

The flowers gossip, oh so sweet,
"Watch out for bees, they move their feet!"
A butterfly flits like a clown,
Dancing high, then tumbling down.

The breeze is ticklish, oh what fun,
It plays with shadows, just on the run.
With every gust, old leaves do sway,
Squirrels yell, "Come join our play!"

Gardens of Gentle Whispers

In the garden, secrets spread,
Carrots giggle, turn to red.
"Why is celery so stiff?"
Lettuce laughs, and gives a riff.

Tulips whisper, 'Who's that guest?'
A butterfly, wearing its best.
"Mind your pollen, it's quite rare!"
"Oops!" it spins—up in the air!

Beetles laugh with tiny funny jokes,
While ants march by, wearing coats.
A ladybug says, "What a treat!"
In this garden, it can't be beat!

Roots of Resilience

Deep in soil, the roots do play,
With tiny friends who dance all day.
"What time is lunch?" a radish cries,
"As soon as we spot the carrots' fries!"

Life's not always a simple race,
But worms groove on, with rhythm and grace.
"We're the backbone of this whole show!"
They wiggle and jive, putting on a glow.

Old oak trees swap tales so grand,
"Remember that time we took a stand?"
With laughter echoing through the grove,
Their roots entwined, a treasure trove.

Verdant Visions

In a forest filled with cheer,
Pine cones chase the squirrels here.
Frogs are croaking, what a sight,
Trying hard to sing tonight.

Bamboo bends with giggling glee,
Leaves whispering jokes to the bee.
Flowers dancing in the breeze,
Telling tales of sneaky mice, please!

A cactus wearing shades, oh wow,
Looks like he's chilling with a cow.
A river chuckles, what a scene,
Splashing its friends — so evergreen!

Under a sky so bold and blue,
Trees are playing peek-a-boo.
Nature's humor makes us smile,
Join the fun, stay for a while!

Song of the Wildflowers

Daisies debating who's the best,
Sunflowers prancing, never rest.
A tulip blushes, says, 'It's me!'
While violets giggle with glee.

Buttercups wear crowns of gold,
Telling stories that never get old.
Bees buzz by with a humorous flit,
Skipping pollen, never to quit.

Garden gnomes doing a jig,
While worms are dancing — isn't that big?
Petunias ponder who's got the flair,
As dandelions float without a care.

The skies echo laughter so light,
As petals twirl in joyful flight.
Nature's party, come take a seat,
Wildflowers' festival can't be beat!

Echoes of Evergreen

Pine trees whispering jokes to the breeze,
While moss giggles, grows under leaves.
Squirrels prance around in a race,
As the winds blow with a woofy grace.

The creek chuckles, splashes around,
Telling secrets without a sound.
A woodpecker's drumming makes all laugh,
Nature's concert, a joyous path!

Fern fronds wave like they're on cue,
Screaming "Hi!" to the sky so blue.
Roots are tickling toes walking near,
The forest's chuckle is so sincere.

Kites of leaves whirl high above,
Nature wraps us in its glove.
In tall trees with laughter so keen,
Life's a party, evergreen!

Caressed by Canopy

In the shade where shadows play,
A squirrel cracks jokes, come what may.
Fungi chuckle, all dressed in brown,
While chipmunks prance around in a crown.

Sunbeams flicker through the leaves,
As nature giggles and never grieves.
A twig breaks — oh! What a surprise!
Bats laugh 'hello' as they arise.

The canopy sways like a gentle rhyme,
Creating humor, stealing time.
Laughter echoes from branch to bough,
Join the forest, take a bow!

Nature's comedy club is loud,
Sharing smiles with every crowd.
Underneath this leafy screen,
Life thrives in such a funny scene!

Graced by Nature's Charm

In a forest full of trees,
Squirrels chatter in the breeze.
Frogs dance in their finest shoes,
While the flowers gossip the news.

Bees are buzzing, oh so bold,
Selling honey, truth be told.
The apples giggle on the vine,
Sharing jokes and sipping wine.

The mushrooms hold a fancy ball,
Toadstools wobble, proud and tall.
A rabbit tries to steal the show,
But trips on roots and falls below.

In this land of green delight,
Everything's a joyful sight.
Laughter echoes, chirps and hops,
A nature fest that never stops.

Colorful Breezes

Winds are tickling my earlobe,
Chasing rainbows, sans a robe.
Dandelions, they take flight,
Spreading laughter, pure delight.

The clouds wear hats, quite absurd,
While a chipmunk starts to herd.
Butterflies in tutu flair,
Twirl and swirl without a care.

A parrot dons a monocle,
With a beak so comical.
It squawks jokes that seem contrived,
Yet it's clear the crowd's alive.

Petunias wink with petals wide,
Daring tulips to take them in stride.
In this carnival of hue,
Nature's jesters, just for you.

The Comfort of Clio

Clio sits under a tree,
Eating snacks, so happily.
She muses on the fluff of clouds,
And giggles with the giggly crowds.

A caterpillar raves and groans,
Complainin' 'bout the weather zones.
While ladybugs on picnic spree,
Count their spots, with utmost glee.

Grasshoppers tell tall tales of fate,
Of their leaps and an odd date.
Clio laughs, it's all a game,
Nature's play, never the same.

So she sprawls on emerald beds,
With dreams of winds and curly heads.
Among the trees, her heart will flow,
In the charm where joy will grow.

Adventures in Green Shadows

In the park, a frog will croak,
Dressed in stripes, a silly joke.
He leaps around with all his might,
Claiming he's a knight tonight.

The grass is soft, a cozy bed,
Where ants hold meetings in their heads.
Twirling leaves just can't keep still,
As critters dance against their will.

A snail declares, "I'm the speed king!"
But his tracks show a lazy fling.
While a wise owl offers rants,
Chiding all the over-ants.

In the shadow of the trees,
Every moment's filled with tease.
Nature's quirks are on parade,
In joy and laughter, unafraid.

The Color of Solace

In a world where broccoli sings,
And carrots wear tiny crowns,
Cabbages roll in their bright green bling,
While spinach twirls, up and down.

Lettuce whispers secrets of joy,
As peas play hopscotch in a line,
Radishes grumble, 'Where's our toy?'
In the garden, everything's fine.

Kale loves to do the cha-cha-chop,
While tomatoes throw salsa like rain,
Cucumbers do the flip-flop hop,
In colors that make the world sane.

So we cheer for this veggie crew,
Each sprout brings laughter, oh so bright,
Who knew greens could be this much fun?
Waving our forks, what a delight!

Symphony of Scented Herbs

In the kitchen, a riot starts,
With basil strumming on a pan,
Rosemary dances, plucking hearts,
And thyme joins in, as only thyme can.

Oregano serenades the stew,
While mint giggles, fresh and spry,
Their zesty tunes just steal the show,
Watch that parsley leap up high!

Sage croons softly to the cheese,
Marjoram's got some funky moves,
A savory symphony, if you please,
Let's get cooking and dance to the grooves!

So next time you chop, don't just slice,
Imagine herbs in grand ballet,
Each little sprig, it feels so nice,
Making dinner, hip-hop hooray!

Meadowspeak

In fields where daisies crack wise,
And buttercups giggle at the sun,
The grass does the twist, what a surprise,
While clovers say, 'Is this a pun?'

Dandelions blow wishes around,
As poppies prance in bright red shoes,
The breeze carries laughter, no one's frowned,
Nature's party is hard to refuse!

Fireflies join; it's a late-night bash,
With crickets providing the sound,
A symphony of sounds, a buzzing clash,
In meadows where joy knows no bound.

So step into this carefree play,
Leave your worries in the dust,
Dance with petals, join the fray,
Enjoy the green — it's a must!

Treetop Murmurs

In the branches, squirrels tell tales,
Of acorns and nutty escapes,
They hop and wiggle in the gales,
While leaves tease with fluttering shapes.

Woodpeckers drum like they're in a band,
While owls chuckle, wise in their roost,
The branches sway like a cool rock stand,
Who knew trees could boast a great boost?

Birds chirp gossip about the sun,
As shadows play tag on the ground,
Even the branches are having fun,
In a foliage retreat where joys abound.

So listen close to the forest's song,
In every rustle, a secret unspools,
For in the green, we all belong,
Nature's laughter is a full set of jewels!

Greenery's Promise

In a garden that sings with hues,
The broccoli jigs with purple shoes.
Carrots debate who has the flair,
While tomatoes laugh without a care.

Frogs in hats hop on the scene,
Chasing dreams in this leafy sheen.
With mushrooms playing hide and seek,
Nature's joke, it's quite unique.

The daisies dance in funny rows,
While rabbits practice their best toes.
Vines twist and twirl, oh what a sight,
In this verde party, pure delight!

So let's toast with sips of dew,
To greens that share a laugh or two.
In this patch, joy's our theme,
Where fun grows high like wildflower dreams.

Unsung Notes of the Grove

In the woods, where giggles sprout,
Squirrels chatter without a doubt.
Bark beetles drum in a groovy beat,
While leaves gossip, oh, what a treat!

Mushrooms mime a comedy show,
While owls laugh, making wisdom glow.
A wisecracking raccoon takes a bow,
As shadows play tricks, and night says wow!

Foxes wear capes, oh so sublime,
While trees tune in to the forest rhyme.
With every rustle and each soft plea,
The unsung notes sing wild and free!

So here's to the grove, a laughing spree,
Where every leaf is wild with glee.
Join in the fun, don't be shy,
In the woodlands, we all can fly!

Musing among Moss and Fern

On the forest floor, mossy fluff reigns,
Where ferns have parties, swapping gains.
Tiny critters in vibrant suits,
Debate the best style of leaf-shaped boots.

The snail's slow dance steals the show,
While caterpillars rock it to and fro.
Laughter echoes through leafy caverns,
As wildflowers joke about the taverns.

Dewdrops giggle, they sparkle and spin,
As sunlight sneaks in with a grin.
With every frolic and every twist,
Nature reminds us: fun's hard to resist!

So skip through the greens with winks and grins,
Absorb the joy that life begins.
Amongst the moss and ferns so spry,
Let's make memories, you and I!

The Language of Leaves

Leaves discuss a wild charade,
In whispers soft, they get cascades.
Each flap and rustle a hilarious joke,
Where even the breeze plays a clever poke.

Branches roll their eyes at the sky,
As clouds drift past with a puffy sigh.
The grass below chuckles in green,
Finding humor in every scene!

The tallest trees make funny faces,
While roots gossip in secret places.
Nature's ensemble, pure delight,
As the wind tickles through with might.

So let's join in, with giggles we land,
In this leafy world, it's simply grand.
With every quip and twist of fate,
In the language of leaves, we celebrate!

Nature's Gentle Embrace

In the park where the squirrels tease,
They race around with such great ease.
I tried to chase, but tripped on grass,
They laughed at me as I went past.

Leaves whisper secrets, soft and light,
A butterfly flirts, oh what a sight.
I sneezed and startled a nearby frog,
He ribbited loud, like a chatty dog.

Clouds play peek-a-boo with the sun,
The flowers giggle, oh what fun!
A picnic spreads out on a big bright quilt,
But ants think it's a party, where's my guilt?

Nature's wonders, so silly and sweet,
Slides in the breeze, oh what a treat!
I dance with daisies, spin around,
Until I trip on roots in the ground.

Exhaling the Wild

A giraffe wears a crown of leafy greens,
While a hippo practices ballet routines.
In the zoo, it's a riotous scene,
The parrots squawk out their jokes, so keen.

A bear tries yoga, it's quite a sight,
Stretching out paws, oh what a plight!
He falls on a log with a goofy thud,
And rolls in the grass like a big brown bud.

Turtles take a break from their slow crawl,
Challenging each other to a footrace, tall.
They jokingly argue who's really fast,
While the rabbits giggle and have a blast.

In the wild, laughter echoes and sings,
Every creature wears its own set of wings.
The sun shines bright, making shadows play,
Funny moments fill the brightening day.

Tides of Green Serenity

Waves of green roll in from the sea,
Where seaweed dances, wild and free.
A crab wears a hat made of coral bright,
While a fish tells jokes with all its might.

The ocean chuckles as we drift by,
Shells are listeners to an oceanic sigh.
Seagulls squawk in a silly parade,
Pursuing a snack that simply won't fade.

Kelp forests sway like they've found a groove,
Fish shimmy along, all making a move.
Jellyfish bop to the music of waves,
While sipping on water as the ocean saves.

Tides ebb and flow with a whispering glee,
Nature's dance carries on joyfully.
A chant of laughter spills from the shore,
As sea stars giggle, who could ask for more?

Verdancy Unfurled

In a garden where eagles like to play,
Flowers bloom in the most odd way.
A tomato wears shades with lively flair,
While cucumbers gossip, oh, do they dare?

The daisies discuss their latest trends,
While the weeds try to make amends.
A sunflower twirls in an elegant pose,
Waving to bees, as they strike a doze.

Chickens in tutus prance about,
As the carrots shout, 'Give us a clout!'
The peppers juggle, handling their spice,
While the zucchini rolls like it's nothing nice.

Verdant laughter fills the air with glee,
Nature's fun surprises, wild and free.
A compost heap grins, proud of its role,
For even it knows how to rock and roll!

Vitality in Shades of Moss

In the forest, a snail on a race,
Zooming slowly with a goofy face.
Moss invites him for a green feast,
Saying, "Just chill, buddy, I'm the yeast!"

Frogs in tuxedos leap with glee,
While toads sing 'cause they're so fancy.
Amidst the twirls of grass and leaf,
A squirrel's dance turns to comic relief.

Mossy carpets stuck on a shoe,
Bouncing in rhythm like they're brand new.
Worms wiggle in time, in stylish dress,
"Cut a rug!" they yell, oh what a mess!

The trees giggle under their coats,
Spreading rumors about silly goats.
Life in green takes a wobbly spin,
Who knew the forest had such thick skin?

Awakening the Earth's Breath

Caterpillars wear glasses, looking smart,
Perched on leaves, they're playing art.
With tiny brushes in their feet,
They paint the world, oh, what a feat!

Bumblebees buzz, producing a tune,
Complaining how flowers are never in bloom.
"Hey, pollen's free!" they shout with flair,
As ants line up like they don't have a care.

Crickets share gossip, pipes in their hands,
Telling tales of their grand summer plans.
"Let's throw a party!" they chirp with pride,
While ladybugs roll by on a wild ride.

The soil cracks jokes, laughing aloud,
Each worm a jester for this vibrant crowd.
Earth's breath tickles, it's time to cheer,
With a wink and a wiggle, it's magic here!

Harvesting the Wind

Dandelions host a windy parade,
Spreading fluff, it's a soft charade.
Their seeds float like wishes, quite absurd,
While bees dance around, singing weird words.

Little squirrels are selling pine cones,
On a corner, they barter and moan.
"Two acorns for a nutty delight!
Come taste our treats, stay for the night!"

The breeze tunes in to this vibrant fair,
As leaves whisper secrets of their affairs.
Each gust giggles with leaves all around,
Joking about the thrill of the ground.

Clouds drift lazily, joining the fun,
While shadows play tag in the setting sun.
In this breezy world where laughter is king,
It's clear that joy makes the heart take wing!

The Dance of Sunlit Ferns

Ferns on a dance floor, twist and twirl,
Each frond in fancy, they all unfurl.
With a backdrop of sunshine, shining bright,
Grasshoppers join in with leaps of delight.

Mushrooms lounge like they're in a spa,
Sipping dew drops, as they sip chai.
"Life's too short!" they cheer with a grin,
As they host a shindig, let the fun begin!

A parade of ants brings a conga line,
Underneath the oaks, all is divine.
With tiny umbrellas and shades so cool,
They strut their stuff; oh, they rule the pool!

In this patchwork of laughter and cheer,
Nature's humor is perfectly clear.
So soak in the sunny, carefree refrain,
With every giggle, we grow and sustain!

Harmonizing with the Green

In the park, a squirrel sings,
Chasing leaves with silly flings.
Grass does giggle, flowers cheer,
Nature's jokes are loud and clear.

Dancing trees in wobbly stance,
Swinging branches, join the dance.
A butterfly in polka-dot,
Whispers secrets, connects the dot.

The brook babbles with a grin,
Tickling rocks, they all join in.
Jumpy toads on lily pads,
Croak the tunes that make us glad.

Clouds roll by with fuzzy heads,
Making shapes like silly spreads.
Sunbeams tickle every face,
Laughter echoes in this space.

Soul of the Serene Woods

In the woods, a chipmunk yawns,
Wearing acorn hats like dawns.
Trees wear coats of leafy grace,
Swaying slow, they find their place.

Mushrooms giggle in a row,
Spinning tales of rain and glow.
A raccoon dances, tries a twirl,
While the wind gives leaves a whirl.

Sticks perform an awkward dance,
Inviting all to take a chance.
The mossy carpet's snug embrace,
Welcomes all to join the race.

Breeze bursts in with silly tunes,
Whirling round beneath the moons.
Nature's laughter fills the air,
As every creature stops to share.

Essence of Emerald

Emerald grass, a jester's hat,
Wobbling ants, now where they're at?
A bumblebee with glasses wide,
Buzzing thoughts, it won't confide.

Leafy gossip in the trees,
Whispering secrets on the breeze.
Insects giggle, patter light,
Throwing parties through the night.

Every flower dons a cape,
In a superhero shape.
Violet tulips wave and sway,
Brightening the dullest day.

Rain splashes down with playful splats,
Puddles form for dancing brats.
Jumping frogs join in the tune,
Underneath the laughing moon.

Dancing through the Foliage

Foliage wiggles in the breeze,
Twirling vines say, "Say, with ease!"
A parrot flaps in rainbow hues,
Throwing jokes in leafy views.

Wobbly woods with socks on trees,
Dancing ants, oh joy, such tease!
A raccoon's moonwalk, what a sight,
Under stars that twinkle bright.

Dandelions play hide and seek,
Telling tales of tiny shrieks.
Petals splash like little paint,
Nature's brush is bold, not faint.

The wind sings, a merry tune,
While frogs croak in perfect croon.
Laughter floats on emerald streams,
Life's a dance, or so it seems.

Nature's Cozy Refuges

In the garden, bugs play tag,
Worms wear shades; they all brag.
Squirrels dance on branches high,
While the daisies watch and sigh.

Rabbits munch on leafy treats,
While snails take their slow walks, neat.
The trees whisper secrets bold,
In the sunlight, tales unfold.

A chipmunk hoards a tiny stash,
While ants march by, oh what a clash!
The birds sing songs that tickle ears,
Echoing forth in fits of cheers.

Even frogs in ponds so swell,
Croak out jokes, do you hear them yell?
Nature's laughter fills the air,
A silly world beyond compare!

The Warmth of Wild Things

Butterflies wear tutus bright,
While bees buzz by, quite a sight.
A hedgehog rolls into a ball,
And giggles, oh so small!

The raccoons have a dance-off soon,
Underneath a cheeky moon.
A skunk shows off its fancy moves,
While everyone else just grooves.

Turtles nap upon a log,
Dreaming sweet of marshy fog.
The yonder breeze plays tricks on hair,
Nature's antics everywhere!

So grab a leaf, let's make some noise,
In this wild place, who needs toys?
Life's a stage, so let it spin,
Surrounded by our nature kin!

Sunlit Sanctuary of Green

In the meadow, frogs wear hats,
Pondering life and seeing bats.
The flowers giggle, oh so spry,
As butterflies dance, floating by.

The sun spills warmth like lemonade,
While bumblebees form a parade.
A cat naps, dreaming of fish,
In the patch of a sunlight wish.

Lizards lounge with swag supreme,
Plotting out their sun-baked scheme.
Clouds, the comedians of the sky,
Dress up as ships sailing high.

Each rustle in grass holds a tale,
Of playful winds on a sunny trail.
Join the fun in this sunny scene,
Where nature laughs, so fresh and clean!

Tranquil Tendrils

Vines tickle trees with a laugh,
While critters use them for a path.
The plants conspire, oh what a plot,
To tickle noses, what a shot!

Lily pads wear crowns of green,
As frogs perform a royal scene.
Meanwhile, ants are busy with chores,
Singing sweet amongst the boars.

The breeze, it sways with a gentle tease,
Carrying scents that aim to please.
The sun's bright smile lights the show,
Watch as nature's antics flow.

So let us frolic in this spree,
Among the vines, wild and free.
A world where laughter takes the stage,
In this green plot, we engage!

Tangled in Green Dreams

In a garden, I tripped on a vine,
Fell face-first into a spinach shrine.
The veggies giggled, what a silly sight,
I swear they whispered, 'Get up, it's light!'

Dancing with carrots, I twirled around,
They chuckled and tumbled, so tightly bound.
Tomatoes blushed, what a jolly crew,
Lettuce leaves laughed, it looked quite absurd too!

With broccoli crowns, we formed a band,
The rhythms of nature, oh how they planned!
We played a tune on some peas in a pod,
When I joined in, they just looked quite odd!

In tangled dreams where veggies convene,
Every hiccup's a comedy scene.
So here's to the plants, so wacky and bright,
In this leafy folly, all feels just right!

Cadence of the Celestial Grove

In the woods, a squirrel started to rap,
Trees swayed along, giving me a clap.
The moon winked down, what a sight to see,
As branches jived in cosmic harmony!

A raccoon beatboxes, what a funny sound,
While owls hoot rhythm, spinning round and round.
The stars twinkle, like they joined the tune,
Even the crickets danced under the moon!

Unicorns in starlight, prancing with flair,
While big-footed legends stomp, without a care.
Leaves twist and twirl, caught up in the beat,
Nature's own rhythm, nothing can compete!

So come join the grove, leave worries behind,
Lose track of time in this joy that we find.
The cadence of laughter fills up the space,
In the whimsy of woods, it's a merry race!

Majestic Shades of Serenity

In a garden cozy, I lay back and sigh,
The daisies debated whether to fly.
Tulips decided to paint the blue sky,
I chuckled aloud, 'Don't let it go dry!'

The sunflowers posed, looking quite grand,
With self-portraits waved in their little plant band.
Petunia stammered, lost in her dreams,
It's a spa day for petals, or so it seems!

Upside down lilies giggled in bloom,
While clovers whispered secrets to the moon.
A dandelion puff took a stupid plunge,
Blowing seeds everywhere, it was pure fun!

Under arching branches, all colors collide,
Nature's parade, what a whimsical ride!
In majestic shades where laughter's the key,
Serenity thrives in pure jollity!

Scent of the Understory

In the underbrush, mushrooms play hide and seek,
While ferns twirl 'round with a squeaky tweak.
The scent of damp earth kicks off a spree,
Every fungus giggles, and joy runs free!

A hedgehog squealed with joy, what a sight,
He rolled on a patch, feeling just right.
The snails had a race, oh what a delight,
Even the roots couldn't help but unite!

Twisting vines joined in, they couldn't resist,
A conga line formed, a dance to assist.
With ladybugs laughing upon every leaf,
Nature's a party, no sign of grief!

So come scent the fun in this lively realm,
In the understory, life takes the helm.
With each funny critter playing their part,
Laughter abounds; it's a botanical art!

Sighs of the Great Outdoors

In the park, I take a leap,
The squirrels give me a cheeky peep.
They chatter loud, like they've no care,
While I trip on soft grass, then stop and stare.

The flowers wink like they're in on a prank,
Bees buzzing by, a truly odd rank.
I laugh when I see a dog on a roll,
Chasing its tail, forgets its control.

A jogger zooms past, but trips on a shoe,
The geese just honk, it's a comical view.
Trees giggle softly, rustling in glee,
"Come join us, mate, you might spill your tea!"

With every inhalation, the world feels so light,
Amidst all the chaos, it feels so right.
In this vibrant circus, I'll dance and I'll hop,
With each silly moment, I'll never stop!

Emerald Currents

In a field, the grass waves, such a funny sight,
Dancing in rhythm, a shimmering light.
There's a breeze that tickles, like a cheeky friend,
Whispering secrets, as nature's trends blend.

A toad in the pond, croaks like an old guy,
Trying to woo frogs, with a croaky sigh.
The lilies float by, in dazzling parade,
Like nature's own jesters, their colors displayed.

The clouds play tag, dodging the sun,
While daisies giggle, "This is such fun!"
I join in the laughter, twirling around,
In this wild escape, joy is unbound.

With every inhale, I taste the delight,
In a world full of antics, everything's bright.
Let's join the fun, in this laughter spree,
With emerald currents, come dance with me!

Fresh Awakening of Flora

Morning light spills like a splash of paint,
Each bloom takes a bow, the shy and the quaint.
A sunflower chuckles at a droopy daff,
"Cheer up, my pal, you're too good for a laugh!"

A butterfly flutters with a zany twist,
Like a flamboyant dancer, it can't be missed.
The petals tell stories of conquering rain,
While weeds have a party, oh, what a gain!

I stumble through ferns, feeling quite spry,
While a ladybug rolls, how high can it fly?
With colors so vivid, it's a sight to behold,
Even the daisies are breaking the mold.

Giggling with flowers, I join the parade,
In this quirky ballet, where laughter is made.
Each breath, a burst of joyful delight,
In this floral festivity, everything's right!

Symphony of the Swaying Trees

The trees are composers, in a giggly mood,
Swirling their branches, with a whimsical brood.
Leaves laugh together, in rustling refrains,
Playing the music of rivers and rains.

A woodpecker drums on a tree with care,
Like a rockstar alive, in the woodland air.
The wind joins the band, with a soft little sigh,
While clouds provide vocals, drifting up high.

Amidst this concert, I find my own tune,
Dancing on roots, beneath the bright moon.
I twirl and I spin, a merry old fool,
While critters applaud with their own brand of cool.

In this symphony grand, with nature so free,
Laughter and music, a vibrant decree.
With every new note, I sing out with glee,
In harmony's arms, it's just you and me!

Breath of the Earth's Heart

In the forest where the ferns dance high,
A squirrel flipped his nut, oh my!
The trees chuckled softly, what a sight,
As leaves wiggled in pure delight.

A chipmunk pranced with such great flair,
Wearing acorns like a hat with care.
The moss giggled underfoot so green,
In this quirky realm, joy reigns supreme.

With every whoosh and rustle near,
The branches whisper, 'Come, have no fear!'
A rabbit in sneakers takes a leap,
While the brook sings a tune, so sweet.

So let's tiptoe through this leafy jest,
And let nature know we think it's the best!
The earth's heart beats, a funny little tune,
Join in the laughter under the moon.

Whimsy in the Wilderness

A bear on a unicycle, what a show!
Balancing honey, oh look at him go!
Raccoons in hats with a flair so grand,
Planning a party for the woodland band.

The owls are DJing, spinning their tracks,
While turtles breakdance, giving no hacks.
A porcupine served snacks on a plate,
While eagles swooped in, looking first-rate.

In this wild circus, laughter is free,
Even the bugs groove, how can that be?
A windy day brings a tumbling tumble,
As leaves join the dance with a playful rumble.

So come out to play where the wild things grow,
Join the merry madness, let your laughter flow.
Each silly moment, a treasure to keep,
In the whimsy of wild, where joy runs deep.

Whispers of Verdant Air

In a jungle where the vines chitchat loud,
A monkey's jig brings out quite the crowd.
Parrots gossip, sharing tales of old,
Each feathered friend, a story to be told.

A frog in a tux, quite dapper and spry,
Leaps to the rhythm, aiming for the sky.
The lilies giggle, floating with grace,
While breezes tickle, a fun little race.

Trees wearing clowns' noses, truly absurd,
Jokes exchanged with each passing bird.
The sun winks down, playing peek-a-boo,
In this botanical circus, laughter ensues.

So let's stroll where the breezes play fair,
And enjoy the riddles whispered in the air.
A concert of chuckles, a nature-made show,
In every green corner, where humor does grow.

Verdure's Caress

Amidst the meadow, a goat in a tie,
Is teaching the daisies how to fly high.
With butterflies laughing as they zoom by,
Nature's own jesters, oh my oh my!

A bear with a broom gives the grass a sweep,
While the dandelions giggle, in a heap.
The sunlight giggles, scattering cheer,
As critters unite in this wild frontier.

The wind plays tunes on the leaves so green,
While worms form a band, quite a lively scene.
Tree trunks are drums as the chorus takes flight,
With humour and love, everything feels right.

So wander this land where laughter resides,
Join in the fun where the green spirit hides.
Each chuckle a gift, each smile a thread,
In verdant embraces, let joy be spread.

The Pulse of Nature

In the forest, trees do sway,
They dance like goofballs all the way.
Squirrels juggle acorns on a spree,
Who knew nature had such comedy?

Bees buzzing loud like they own the place,
Wearing tiny goggles, a perfect case.
Turtles slow-dance, no rush in sight,
While rabbits hop, oh what a flight!

Mushrooms giggle in the rainy haze,
Fungi parties for days and days.
The sun peeks in with a wink and grin,
Nature's laugh track, let the fun begin!

So if you're feeling down and grim,
Just take a stroll where the lights are dim.
Nature's humor, wild and free,
Is the best medicine, don't you agree?

Emerald Exhalation

The grass tickles toes with a soft caress,
Clouds are marshmallows, I must confess.
The wind whispers jokes in a playful tone,
Makes me giggle, never alone.

Lawn gnomes gossip under starry lights,
With silly hats, they have wild nights.
Raccoons steal snacks with crafty flair,
While frogs croak tunes without a care.

Dandelions puff like a blown-up cake,
Games of hide-and-seek they partake.
The trees snicker as I trip and fall,
Nature's playground is the best of all!

So let the leaves flutter like laughter's sound,
In every corner, joy will be found.
In the emerald fields, life's a show,
Let's make it funny, let's let it flow!

Where Hope Takes Root

In a garden where the wild things grow,
We plant our dreams in a row.
A carrot wears shades and looks quite cool,
While cabbages chat by the garden pool.

Sunflowers stand tall with a cheeky grin,
Taking selfies with bees, counting to ten.
The zucchini pranks with a sly little twist,
Sending out seedlings, I can't resist.

Butterflies flutter in a fashion show,
Wearing the colors, putting on a glow.
The compost heap tells tales of the past,
Whispered secrets that seem to last.

So if you find yourself feeling low,
Just plant a seed, give it a go.
In the heart of the garden, hope takes its flight,
With a sprinkle of humor, everything's right!

Lush Dreams in Springtime

Spring arrives with a silly hat,
Dancing around like a playful cat.
Flowers burst out in laugh-out-loud hues,
"Check out my color!" they seem to muse.

Bees have banded together for a song,
In the blooms, they buzz all day long.
Worms wiggle in the soil with glee,
Saying, "Look at us, come dance with me!"

The rain drops down like comedy gold,
Turning puddles into stories bold.
Kites fly high, with dreams attached,
While clouds play hide and seek, all matched.

So when spring pokes you with sunshine bright,
Join the laughter, feel the light.
In the lush and lively, put on a grin,
For in nature's riddle, fun begins!

The Language of Foliage

In the forest, leaves have much to say,
Whispering secrets in a leafy ballet.
Branches giggle, rustling with glee,
Talking about squirrels and their acorn spree.

Mossy carpets tickle your toes,
While the old oak tree laughs at woes.
Sprouts joke about being small and green,
Dreaming of heights they'll one day glean.

Pinecones and twigs share their wise lore,
While ferns wiggle like they're on the dance floor.
The breeze catches it all, a comedic show,
Nature's stand-up on the forest floor.

Overhead, birds chirp, making a scene,
Complaining about the state of their cuisine.
Leaves sigh, rolling their chlorophyll eyes,
As another squirrel steals their sweet fries.

Beneath the Verdant Veil

Under leafy umbrellas, the critters convene,
Chirping and clucking, it's quite the routine.
Turtles take bets on who'll win the race,
While rabbits doubt the slowpoke's pace.

Frogs in tuxedos leap to the floor,
Dancing for lady frogs, always wanting more.
A snail, quite smug, moves oh-so-slow,
Claiming he's winning the beauty show.

Sunbeams peek in—what a delightful sight!
Animate forms prance, creating delight.
The grass laughs softly, a ticklish affair,
As daisies gossip, spreading joy in the air.

The canopy chuckles, holding the score,
As laughter unites every frog, leaf, and spore.
Nature's jesters, in this green domain,
Making every day feel like a circus refrain.

Caresses from the Canopy

Sunlight filters through branches like sprinkles of fun,
Beaming on flowers, giddy under the sun.
Leaves dangle down, giving high-fives to bees,
While ants parade, waving with ease.

The wind takes a break, just to join in the dance,
Pulling at petals, giving blossoms a chance.
Ladybugs chuckle, all spots and no cares,
Flitting through laughter, floating like flares.

Crickets tell tales of the night's quiet thrills,
While mushrooms plot paths by the hillside hills.
With jokes so corny, they wrap plants in mirth,
Dancing with daisies, a celebration of earth.

As shadows grow long, the fun doesn't wane,
Every creature alive joins in the refrain.
Nature's embrace, unexpected and bright,
Caresses from above in pure delight.

A Breath of Renewal

In a cycle of giggles, the seasons collide,
Flowers burst out, they cannot hide.
Pollinators buzzing with jokes so absurd,
As blossoms shake petals—it's all a bit blurred.

Winter whispers gossip, trying to tease,
While spring acts all fluffy, spreading its ease.
Summer bounces in, all tan and resplendent,
With a smile wide enough to be truly transcendent.

Autumn arrives, dropping leaves with flair,
Waving 'goodbye' but knows we still care.
In every turn, there's mischief anew,
Nature's punchlines woven in dew.

So laugh with the blossoms, join the green throng,
For every little moment, we all belong.
In this playful world, we're free to unveil,
A breath of pure joy in nature's grand tale.

Canvas of Canopy

Leaves tickle the sun, and they laugh
Swaying like dancers, in the midday bath.
Clouds might get jealous, they drift and they pout,
While trees throw a party, no doubt, no doubt!

Squirrels in tuxedos prepare for a show,
Chasing their nuts, putting on a grand flow.
The branches are their stage, the roots are their scene,
In this leafy theater, life's silly and keen.

Birds wear bright hats, and they sing out in cheer,
A chorus of chirps that everyone hears.
But don't ask the sloth, he's stuck in his seat,
He's part of the act—who said that ain't sweet?

Sunbeams peek through, like kids playing hide,
Up in the treetops, joy cannot abide.
With laughter a'ringing, no gloom can intrude,
In this lively forest, it's fun that's renewed!

Flourish of the Foliage

Ferns wear green glasses, trees wear a grin,
All the plants gossip about who will win.
In the big plant contest, who'll grow the most wide?
The daisies keep laughing, while roses take pride.

Running vines twist together, a tricky old maze,
While cacti aim for the tallest of praise.
The daisies and dandelions go head-to-head,
Who will sprout first? Place your bets and be fed!

Sunflowers struttin', they turn with a glee,
They get all the rays, reclining with tea.
But hollyhocks rise, with a theatrical flair,
Bringing everyone joy, with their cousin, the air.

Pollen is dancing like confetti on air,
Bees buzzing along, to join in the fair.
With all this green mischief, who needs a crown?
In the garden's gala, we all get to clown!

Lush Harmonies

In the garden where giggles grow wild, oh my,
Petunias and pansies wave blossoms to the sky.
The ants throw a parade, on tiny big feet,
Celebrating the wonders of life, oh so sweet!

Bees bounce like jesters, up high and down low,
Collecting their treasures while putting on a show.
Each bloom tells a story, each stem shares a jest,
In this playful patch where nature's impressed.

The daisies do cartwheels, with clumsy delight,
While mushrooms hold parties all through the night.
With each passing breeze, a tickle and cheer,
Nature's sweet orchestra is all we hold dear.

As the stars twinkle softly, in gardens they dance,
To the music of leaves, join in the romance.
From roots to the tips, they unite to enthrall,
In this lush harmonies, there's laughter for all!

Joy of Growing Things

With sprouts poking out, like they're playing a game,
The veggies go wild, hopping around, what a fame!
Lettuce is giggling, and carrots are sly,
While radishes blush, hiding under the sky.

Potatoes play tag, scooting deep in the earth,
Mocking the beans that brag 'bout their worth.
Each seed has a dream, with each raindrop a cheer,
In this merry garden, they banish all fear.

The chard's in a tutu, just ready to dance,
While tomatoes roll by in an innocent prance.
They make quite the racket, those rows of delight,
In the garden of laughter, everything feels right.

Oh, the joy of growing, a riot with sun,
It's a wacky affair, never to outrun.
Nature's own canvas, painted all in fun,
With smiles sprouting up until the day's done!

Quietude in the Canopy

In the trees, a squirrel prances,
Chasing shadows, taking chances.
With acorns dropping like raindrops,
He giggles, then suddenly stops.

A sloth hangs upside down, so chill,
He yawns, just going in for the thrill.
'Hey look,' he says, 'I'm a bat!'
The others laugh; that's where he's at.

The parrot squawks in endless chatter,
Claiming that he's the best at flatter.
He talks to leaves, they shake and sway,
'You're the best, I must say!'

Through branches, the sun streams bright,
Creating scenes of pure delight.
In the canopy, life's a jest,
Nature's humor, we can't contest.

Essence of Earth's Palette

A daisy talked to a big, red rose,
'Dude, what's with your fancy clothes?'
The rose replied, with poise and flair,
'It's fashion week, I must prepare!'

The sunflowers tower, so very tall,
'More sunlight, please!' they call.
While the tulips shiver in their shoes,
'We prefer a little rain, thank you blues.'

The daisies dance in a wondrous line,
Shaking their heads, feeling divine.
They twirl and swirl in a vibrant jest,
Nature's colors, always dressed best.

Painted insects take their flight,
Playing hide and seek, what a sight!
Their hues a riot, so surreal,
Earth's palette, a whimsical deal.

Vibrant Echoes of the Wild

In the woods, the fox makes a pose,
'Am I cute?' he asks the crows.
They cackle back with raucous glee,
'You're more of a joke, wait and see!'

The deer prances with flair so grand,
Claiming, 'I'm a unicorn, understand?'
The rabbits giggle, rolling around,
'With that horn? You're upside-down!'

The owls hoot out riddles at night,
'What's green and sings? Give it a bite!'
With crickets chirping their nightly tune,
Even the moon chuckles, a buffoon.

The wildflowers whisper, 'We're all the rage,'
Flaunting their hues on Nature's stage.
In the wild, the fun never ends,
Laughter frolics—our furry friends!

Living Breath of the Meadow

The grass tickles the toes of wandering feet,
While ants decide to host a grand feast.
'Pass the crumbs!' they squeak with delight,
'Oh wait, is that a butterfly in flight?'

The daisies wave, trying to be heard,
'We're prettier than the crazy bird!'
The robin laughs, 'Well, I can sing,'
And flies around with a boisterous ring.

In the breeze, the grasses sway,
'We're here for the dance, hip-hip-hooray!'
A bumblebee joins, buzzing along,
'This meadow life is where I belong.'

The sun sets low, painting the sky,
While flowers yawn and say goodbye.
In the meadow, laughter's the seed,
Each moment cherished, a joyful need.

Green Canopy Conversations

In the trees, squirrels chatter loud,
Chatting secrets, oh so proud.
"Did you see that bird?" one tree said,
"He tripped on a twig and fell on his head!"

Frogs are croaking, bass lines strong,
They debate all night, never wrong.
"Your croak is flat!" a frog will tease,
"At least I don't hop with such wobbly knees!"

Leaves rustle gossip, whispers flow,
"Did you hear about the mushroom show?"
"I heard it's wild, with toadstool style!"
"Let's dress the moss, make it worthwhile!"

Bugs join in, buzzing with glee,
"Is that a dance?" "No, it's a spree!"
Grasses sway with a giggly squirm,
Nature's mischief, full of charm.

Nature's Rhythm

The wind whistled tunes in a silly way,
Making branches swing, come out and play!
"Is that a breeze?" a butterfly cried,
"Or just the trees laughing, full of pride?"

Clouds shaped like llamas float by with flair,
While daisies dance, without a care.
"Hey flower, stop faking – that's not a jig!"
"Oh hush! Just because you're a little twig!"

Ants marching on, a tiny parade,
Strutting like stars, as if they were made.
"Look at my groove!" one boldly claimed,
"You're all a bunch of critters, a little too tamed!"

Nature giggles, we join the fun,
Yelling "Yeah!" till the day is done.
With every rustle, and every hum,
Life's a fiesta, full of drum.

The Poetry of Pollinators

Bees writing verses in nectar's glow,
Buzzing about, they're putting on a show.
"Is this a flower or a sweet buffet?"
"I'll try them all, then nap through the day!"

Butterflies compete with colors so bright,
Flapping 'round like they own the night.
"What's your style?" one asked with glee,
"I'm all about spots, how about thee?"

Ladybugs roll in with a smile that's wide,
"Let's have a party, let's not hide!"
They dance on leaves, a polka so sweet,
"Just don't squish us, it's quite the feat!"

Pollinators buzz in delightful spree,
Crafting a world, so wild and free.
With laughter in pollen, they twirl like stars,
Turning the garden into a bazaar!

Embracing the Essence of Mother Earth

Oh, Mother Earth, with your playful tricks,
You hide your treasures with giggles and kicks.
"Where's the sunshine?" a daisy asked,
"Under my blanket! I'm here to bask!"

The rocks taped a sign, "Beach chairs ahead!"
While mossy cushions told tales in bed.
"I'm napping!" croaked a turtle in view,
"Please don't disturb; it's my sleepy brew."

Trees throw shade as they host a bash,
Inviting the critters for a fun-filled splash.
"Pass the acorns! Let's party all day!"
As branches waved to join in the play.

With laughter so hearty, the blossoms hum,
"Let's make a wish while the bugs all drum!"
In this wild nature, absurd and free,
We find joy abundant, can't you see?

www.ingramcontent.com/pod-product-compliance
Lightning Source LLC
Chambersburg PA
CBHW070314120526
44590CB00017B/2669